Cars

Transportation Machines

At Work

By Hal Rogers

The Child's World®, Inc.

Published by The Child's World®, Inc.
PO Box 326
Chanhassen, MN 55317-0326
800-599-READ
www.childsworld.com

Design and Production:
The Creative Spark, San Juan Capistrano, CA

Photos: © 2000 David M. Budd Photography: cover, 5, 6, 9, 10, 13, 14, 15, 17, 19, 21, 23
        © Reuters NewMedia Inc./CORBIS: 7

Library of Congress Cataloging-in-Publication Data

Rogers, Hal, 1966-
        Cars / by Hal Rogers.
            p. cm.
        ISBN 1-56766-964-6
        1. Automobiles—Juvenile literature. [1. Automobiles.] I. Title.
TL206 .R64 2001
629.222—dc21

                                                    00-011373

Contents

On the Job

On the job, cars carry people from place to place. Some people take their cars to work. Other people drive their cars for fun.

Some people like fancy sports
cars. They can go very fast!

Race car drivers speed around a race track. But driving fast can be dangerous. People who drive on the road obey the **speed limit.**

Police officers drive special cars. Their cars have **sirens** that make loud noises. They also have bright lights that flash. Sirens and lights let other drivers know the police car is coming.

What do people do if they don't have a car? They can take a taxi. **Passengers** pay a taxi driver to take them where they want to go.

Some cars can go on rough roads.

People drive them in the mountains

and the country.

The driver and one passenger sit in the front seats. Other passengers sit in the back. Babies and small children sit in special car seats. Everyone in a car should wear a **seat belt.**

Many cars have a **trunk.** People can put suitcases in it when they take a trip. They can also carry shopping bags or sports gear in it.

Cars have special lights. They have white **headlights** on the front. They have red **taillights** on the back. Lights help drivers see at night. They also help other people see a car when it's dark outside.

Climb Aboard!

Would you like to see where the driver sits? The driver uses a steering wheel to drive the car. Cars have **controls.** One control turns on the lights. Another tells the driver how fast she is going. Mirrors let the driver see other cars behind her. **Pedals** on the floor make the car stop and go. The driver looks through a big window called a **windshield.**

Up Close

The inside

1. The windshield

2. The mirrors

3. The steering wheel

4. The controls

5. The pedals

6. The seat

The outside

1. The wheels

2. The doors

3. The windshield

4. The headlights

5. The trunk

6. The taillights

Glossary

controls (kun-TROLZ)
Controls are buttons, switches, and other tools that make a machine work. A driver uses controls to drive a car.

headlights (HED-lytz)
Headlights are bright lights on the front of a car. Drivers use headlights to help them see at night.

passengers (PASS-en-jerz)
Passengers are travelers in vehicles such as cars, airplanes, or buses. Taxis carry passengers from place to place.

pedals (PED-ulz)
Pedals are controls that people work with their feet. Pedals on the floor make the car stop and go.

seat belt (SEET BELT)
A seat belt is a strap attached to the seat of a car. Seat belts hold people in their seats in case of a crash or a jolt.

sirens (SY-renz)
Sirens are horns that make very loud noises. Police cars have sirens to warn other drivers that they are coming.

speed limit (SPEED LIM-it)
A speed limit is a law that tells drivers how fast they can go. Drivers must obey the speed limit.

taillights (TALE-lytz)
Taillights are bright red lights on the back of a car. At night, drivers watch for the taillights of cars in front of them.

trunk (TRUNK)
A trunk is a place in the back of a car where people can store things. Most cars have trunks.

windshield (WIND-sheeld)
A windshield is a window on the front of a car. The driver looks through the windshield.